THE OFFICIAL NEWCASTLE UNITED FC ANNUAL 2013

Written by Mark Hannen
Designed by Chris Dalrymple

A Grange Publication

© 2012. Published by Grange Communications Ltd., Edinburgh, under licence from Newcastle United Football Club. Printed in the EU.

Thanks to Dan Sheridan, Michael Bolam and Paul Joannou.

Photographs © Ian Horrocks and Serena Taylor.

ISBN 978-1-908925-11-4

Contents

Welcome from Alan Pardew

It is my pleasure to once again welcome you to the Official 2013 Newcastle United Annual, packed as usual with plenty of exciting and interesting features as well as some brilliant photographs which spectacularly capture some of last season's outstanding action.

Turning briefly to last year, great credit is due to the players for what was a tremendous effort in securing a fifth place finish for the club. We started the season well, kept it going mid-season despite a few hiccups along the way and then ended in fine style, including a six match winning run that helped propel us into the Europa League.

So this season our challenge is to maintain the high standards we set ourselves during the 2011/12 campaign whilst we set our stall out to challenge on four fronts, primarily the Premier League, but also the two domestic Cups which we're very keen to make an impact on this season and of course Europe where we haven't played since 2007.

Nothing could be achieved at this club without the fantastic support we have had from you the fans and for that, I and the players are eternally grateful. Your love for the game coupled with the noise, passion and fervour we experience, home and away, is genuinely second to none.

This Annual is a tremendous read and I hope you enjoy it. Telling the story of last season, it also relives the memorable goals we scored, looks back on our great history and also includes a good mix of fun quizzes and crosswords to test your knowledge.

With very best wishes.

Alan Pardew
Team Manager

A SEASON TO REMEMBER

After consolidating their place in the Premier League in the 2010/11 season, United's aim last season was to push on and try and secure a top half finish. That they did in fine style, but it was much better than that, never out of the top seven all season a final finishing position of fifth, and Europa League qualification, was an exceptional achievement.

AUGUST

Pl	W	D	L	F	A	Pts	Pos
3	2	1	0	3	1	7	6

The fixture list had thrown up a challenging pair of games to get Newcastle's league campaign underway, with the opening day visit of Champions League regulars Arsenal followed by a trip to neighbours Sunderland. A lively encounter ended 0-0 at St. James' Park, despite plenty of action and incident, the main talking point coming when striker Gervinho was shown a red card after a scuffle with Barton. Seven days later, the fixture that fans had waited all summer for finally arrived, with the 145th Tyne-Wear derby played in front of almost 48,000 at an expectant Stadium of Light. In a game of few clear-cut chances, it was Ryan Taylor who provided the game's defining moment, bending a delightful free-kick into the top corner, etching himself into Geordie folklore. A Carling Cup win at Scunthorpe followed before the month was rounded off in positive fashion with a 2-1 victory over Fulham on Tyneside – a win, thanks to a brace from Leon Best, that left the Magpies in the top six.

SEPTEMBER

Pl	W	D	L	F	A	Pts	Pos
6	3	3	0	7	3	12	4

After a successful start to the new campaign that had seen United take seven points from a possible nine and progress to the third round of the Carling Cup, September posed a new set of challenges for Alan Pardew's men. Their first game of the month following an international break was a tricky-looking trip to newly-promoted Queens Park Rangers where a goalless draw was secured. The Toon Army then descended on Birmingham for another tough game away at Aston Villa and despite the points being shared once more following a 1-1 scoreline, with Leon Best netting, this was a tale of what might have been - former favourite Shay Given keeping out a superb Yohan Cabaye strike at the death. Changes were made to the starting XI for the Carling Cup trip to Nottingham Forest three days later where United won a thriller 4-3. After no goals in his first five games for the Club, Demba Ba chose the home game with Blackburn Rovers to announce his arrival – and announce it he did, with a devastating 27-minute hat-trick, United winning 3-1 and moving up to fourth.

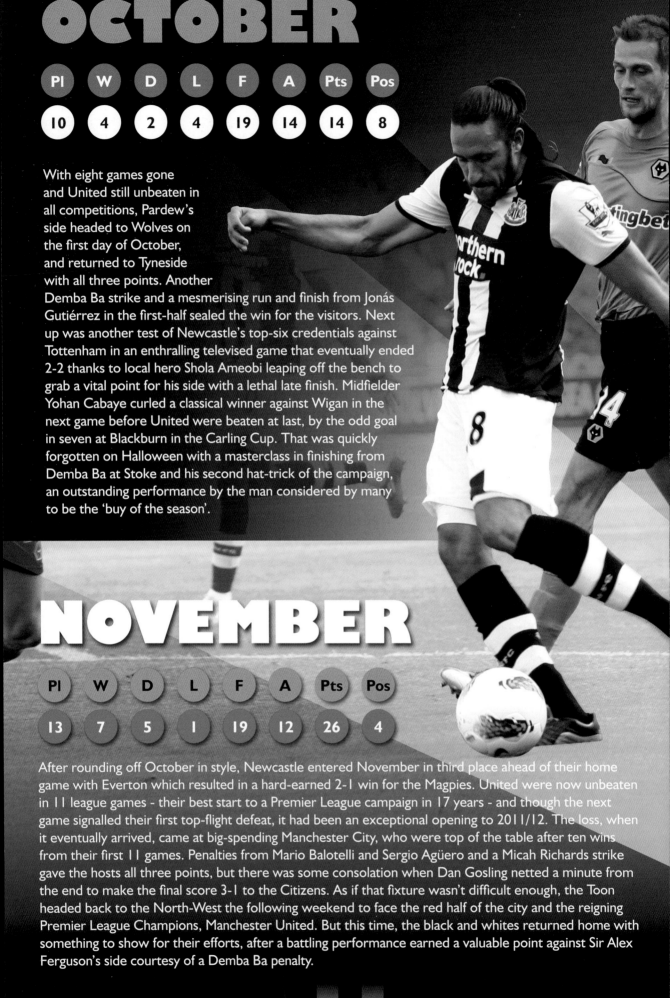

OCTOBER

Pl	W	D	L	F	A	Pts	Pos
10	4	2	4	19	14	14	8

With eight games gone and United still unbeaten in all competitions, Pardew's side headed to Wolves on the first day of October, and returned to Tyneside with all three points. Another Demba Ba strike and a mesmerising run and finish from Jonás Gutiérrez in the first-half sealed the win for the visitors. Next up was another test of Newcastle's top-six credentials against Tottenham in an enthralling televised game that eventually ended 2-2 thanks to local hero Shola Ameobi leaping off the bench to grab a vital point for his side with a lethal late finish. Midfielder Yohan Cabaye curled a classical winner against Wigan in the next game before United were beaten at last, by the odd goal in seven at Blackburn in the Carling Cup. That was quickly forgotten on Halloween with a masterclass in finishing from Demba Ba at Stoke and his second hat-trick of the campaign, an outstanding performance by the man considered by many to be the 'buy of the season'.

NOVEMBER

Pl	W	D	L	F	A	Pts	Pos
13	7	5	1	19	12	26	4

After rounding off October in style, Newcastle entered November in third place ahead of their home game with Everton which resulted in a hard-earned 2-1 win for the Magpies. United were now unbeaten in 11 league games - their best start to a Premier League campaign in 17 years - and though the next game signalled their first top-flight defeat, it had been an exceptional opening to 2011/12. The loss, when it eventually arrived, came at big-spending Manchester City, who were top of the table after ten wins from their first 11 games. Penalties from Mario Balotelli and Sergio Agüero and a Micah Richards strike gave the hosts all three points, but there was some consolation when Dan Gosling netted a minute from the end to make the final score 3-1 to the Citizens. As if that fixture wasn't difficult enough, the Toon headed back to the North-West the following weekend to face the red half of the city and the reigning Premier League Champions, Manchester United. But this time, the black and whites returned home with something to show for their efforts, after a battling performance earned a valuable point against Sir Alex Ferguson's side courtesy of a Demba Ba penalty.

NEWCASTLE UNITED

Pl	W	D	L	F	A	Pts	Pos
19	8	6	5	26	25	30	7

Ahead of the final month of 2012, the footballing world was shaken by the devastating news of former Newcastle star Gary Speed's death. The midfielder made 285 appearances for the Club and was just 42-years-old. United hosted Chelsea on the first weekend of December and although an away win resulted, things could have been very different had the early card shown to Blues defender David Luiz been red instead of yellow after a foul on Demba Ba. The game also saw Steven Taylor ruled out for the rest of the season with a ruptured Achilles. A wounded United then suffered another defeat away at newly-promoted Norwich City seven days later before two pre-Christmas fixtures in four days at the Sports Direct Arena offered Pardew's players the chance to get back on track, but there wasn't much festive cheer on offer after clashes with Swansea and West Brom delivered only a single point. There was to be some holiday joy, however, with a trip to Bolton on Boxing Day where quick-fire goals from Ba and Ben Arfa registered United's first win in seven games. But the Toon came back down to earth with a bump just days later when a brace from former striker Craig Bellamy helped hand Liverpool a 3-1 win at Anfield.

JANUARY

Pl	W	D	L	F	A	Pts	Pos
22	10	6	6	32	30	36	6

If December had been a testing month for Newcastle, January was to get the new year off to an absolute flyer. Champions Manchester United arrived and in front of a sell-out crowd and millions watching worldwide on television, Alan Pardew's men produced arguably their best performance of the season to win 3-0. Three days later Hatem Ben Arfa produced a mesmerising solo effort to help United through in the FA Cup against Blackburn. A hat-trick of new year home fixtures was completed the following weekend when QPR were sent packing thanks to a super Leon Best strike. United had responded well to a disappointing December, and had forced their way back into the top six, but a set-back was on the horizon away at Fulham. Having dominated the game during the opening 45-minutes United collapsed after the break in a game that eventually ended 5-2 to the Londoners. And worse was to follow in the South-East the following weekend when a goal from Will Buckley was enough to see Championship side Brighton dump United out of the FA Cup.

FEBRUARY

Pl	W	D	L	F	A	Pts	Pos
26	12	7	7	38	38	43	6

Mid-way through January, Alan Pardew had secured his one and only signing of the winter window, but as the remainder of the season would prove, it was no ordinary transfer with Senegal striker Papiss Cissé being handed the famous number nine shirt. February got underway with a trip to face an in-form Blackburn Rovers side at Ewood Park but in a classic smash and grab, the Toon took all three points thanks to an own-goal from Scott Dann and a late strike from Gabriel Obertan, with a crucial penalty save from Tim Krul sandwiched in between. The match with Aston Villa at the Sports Direct Arena four days later began with Cissé on the bench, but an injury to Leon Best saw the forward make an earlier-than-expected appearance and his dream debut was capped with a wonderful arrowed strike into the top corner to hand Newcastle a 2-1 win. An evening to forget was had at Tottenham Hotspur the following weekend, as Harry Redknapp's side thrashed United 5-0 but their top-six spot was cemented before the month was out with a 2-2 draw with struggling Wolverhampton Wanderers.

MARCH

Pl	W	D	L	F	A	Pts	Pos
30	14	8	8	44	42	50	6

The small matter of the 146th Tyne-Wear derby got the month of March underway, and as the game moved into stoppage time, it looked for all the world like Martin O'Neill's Black Cats would claim the bragging rights. Demba Ba had missed a spot-kick with eight minutes to go but in a frantic finale, Geordie pride was restored when Shola Ameobi was on hand to score at the far post, his seventh career goal against the red and whites. Newcastle headed to North London eight days later for a top-six clash with Arsène Wenger's Arsenal but this time it was Thomas Vermaelen, who scored the winner with virtually the last kick of the game. It was an agonising defeat for the Magpies, but Pardew's men bounced back with a narrow home victory over Norwich, Papiss Cissé scoring early on, which lit the fuse paper on an incredible run of six wins on the trot. And the insatiable number nine was at it again the following weekend in a devastating first-half performance at West Brom that saw the Toon play some of their best football of the campaign. In a blistering spell, Cissé (2) and Hatem Ben Arfa put United three up in the first 34 minutes and that was game over.

APRIL

Pl	W	D	L	F	A	Pts	Pos
35	18	8	9	53	46	62	5

With eight games to go, and with Pardew's side sitting in sixth place in the table, their European credentials were put to the test with the visit of Liverpool on April Fools' Day. It was an uncomfortable return for the former Toon duo of Andy Carroll and José Enrique, as that man Cissé kept his incredible scoring run going with his second brace in a row. His goalscoring exploits continued in South Wales against Swansea on Good Friday, and another finishing masterclass - and yet another double from the forward - secured a fourth victory in a row. The Magpies were now in top gear and with two home games in a row to come, confidence was high sky high. A stunning individual goal from Ben Arfa changed the course of the first of those games against struggling Bolton Wanderers, and who else but Cissé put the result beyond doubt. And against Stoke 12 days later, it was the turn of Cabaye to remind the Toon faithful of his undoubted talent, scoring twice in a 3-0 win. The wheels came off at Wigan before the month of March was out following a shock 4-0 defeat, but as the final three games of the season approached, Newcastle found themselves competing for a top four finish and a place in the Champions League.

MAY

NEWCASTLE UNITED

Pl	W	D	L	F	A	Pts	Pos
38	19	8	11	56	51	65	5

As May arrived, Newcastle were all but guaranteed a European place ahead of their last three fixtures. First up was a Chelsea side that had overcome the mighty Barcelona the previous week but what unfolded was a memorable night for the Toon. Papiss Cissé had already made headlines in spectacular fashion, with eight goals in his previous seven games, but even by his standards he raised the bar to incredible heights in West London. His first was outstanding but his second 'deep into injury time' would make waves across the footballing world as one of the greatest goals in Premier League history. Four days after that 2-0 win, Manchester City arrived on Tyneside with the destiny of the title still to be decided. City duly delivered, scoring twice in the last 20 minutes through Yaya Touré, but not before the Magpies gave them a real run for their money. Before the final game of the campaign, Liverpool's midweek win over Chelsea at Anfield secured fifth-place for Newcastle and though the final day saw Alan Pardew's class of 2012 lose 3-1 at Everton, nothing could dampen the feeling of elation as a place in the Europa League was confirmed. To crown what had been an incredible season, captain Fabricio Coloccini was named in the PFA's Team of the Season and Pardew's efforts were rewarded twice, with the Toon boss landing the Barclays Premier League and League Managers Association's Manager of the Year awards.

Season Statistics 2011/12

	League	FA Cup	Lge Cup	2011/12	Total NUFC
Mehdi ABEID	0 (0) 0	1 (0) 0	1 (0) 0	2 (0) 0	2 (0) 0
Sammy AMEOBI	1 (9) 0	0 (0) 0	0 (3) 1	1 (12) 1	1 (13) 1
Shola AMEOBI	8 (19) 2	1 (1) 0	0 (1) 0	9 (21) 2	193 (140) 72
Demba BA	32 (2) 16	0 (0) 0	2 (0) 0	34 (2) 16	34 (2) 16
Joey BARTON	2 (0) 0	0 (0) 0	0 (0) 0	2 (0) 0	69 (15) 8
Hatem BEN ARFA	16 (10) 5	2 (0) 1	2 (0) 0	20 (10) 6	23 (11) 7
Leon BEST	16 (2) 4	2 (0) 0	1 (0) 0	19 (2) 4	35 (11) 10
Papiss CISSÉ	13 (1) 13	0 (0) 0	0 (0) 0	13 (1) 13	13 (1) 13
Yohan CABAYE	34 (0) 4	2 (0) 0	2 (0) 1	38 (0) 5	38 (0) 5
Fabricio COLOCCINI	35 (0) 0	1 (0) 0	3 (0) 1	39 (0) 1	154 (0) 5
Rob ELLIOT	0 (0) 0	0 (0) 0	1 (0) 0	1 (0) 0	1 (0) 0
Shane FERGUSON	0 (7) 0	0 (1) 0	1 (0) 0	1 (8) 0	6 (12) 0
Dan GOSLING	1 (10) 1	0 (2) 0	2 (0) 0	3 (12) 1	3 (13) 1
Danny GUTHRIE	13 (3) 1	1 (0) 0	2 (0) 1	16 (3) 2	92 (12) 9
Jonás GUTIÉRREZ	37 (0) 2	2 (0) 1	1 (0) 0	40 (0) 3	136 (17) 10
Tim KRUL	38 (0) 0	2 (0) 0	2 (0) 0	42 (0) 0	73 (3) 0
Peter LØVENKRANDS	2 (7) 0	0 (0) 0	2 (1) 3	4 (8) 3	55 (30) 29
Sylvain MARVEAUX	1 (6) 0	0 (0) 0	3 (0) 0	4 (6) 0	4 (6) 0
Gabriel OBERTAN	18 (5) 1	1 (0) 0	0 (2) 0	19 (7) 1	19 (7) 1
James PERCH	13 (12) 0	1 (0) 0	2 (0) 0	16 (12) 0	27 (16) 0
Davide SANTON	19 (5) 0	2 (0) 0	1 (0) 0	22 (5) 0	22 (5) 0
Danny SIMPSON	35 (0) 0	2 (0) 0	3 (0) 1	40 (0) 1	112 (0) 2
Alan SMITH	0 (2) 0	0 (0) 0	0 (0) 0	0 (2) 0	77 (17) 0
Ryan TAYLOR	23 (7) 2	0 (2) 0	1 (0) 1	24 (9) 3	62 (25) 9
Steven TAYLOR	14 (0) 0	0 (0) 0	0 (1) 0	14 (1) 0	188 (14) 13
Cheick TIOTÉ	24 (0) 0	0 (0) 0	0 (0) 0	24 (0) 0	50 (2) 1
Haris VUČKIÉ	2 (2) 0	0 (0) 0	0 (1) 0	2 (3) 0	6 (6) 0
Mike WILLIAMSON	21 (1) 0	2 (0) 0	1 (0) 0	24 (1) 0	70 (3) 0

In addition, the following players made the matchday 18 but never got off the bench during 2011/12: Fraser Forster, Paul Dummett, Steve Harper, Jeff Henderson, Ole Söderberg and James Tavernier.

Classic Clashes

Newcastle United have been involved in many memorable and outstanding matches in their history. Some are labelled 'great' because of the excitement generated, some by their significance and some by the terrific football played and quality of the goals scored.

Games such as the 5–0 hammering of Manchester United in 1996 and the 3–2 defeat of Barcelona in 1997 will always be high on the list, hence their inclusion in previous Annuals, but we can't let events of last season go unreported so here we relive two marvellous occasions, the visit of Manchester United to Tyneside and United's win at Stamford Bridge, their first in the Premier League.

Both games will be remembered for years to come, the fantastic football, the goals in each game and the unique crackling atmosphere the Geordie supporters generate at home and away.

JANUARY 4TH 2012
PREMIER LEAGUE
NEWCASTLE UNITED 3
MANCHESTER UNITED 0

The year 2012 got off to the best possible start with a memorable 3-0 home victory over Manchester United - the Magpies' first victory over the Red Devils since September 2001 when the black 'n' whites ran out 4–3 winners in a game remembered by many for Roy Keane's tangle with Alan Shearer and the red card that came the Irishman's way. Newcastle dominated proceedings throughout the entire 90 minutes, with Demba Ba and Yohan Cabaye finding the back of the net before a Phil Jones own goal completed the scoring right at the death. The deadlock was broken by Demba Ba in the 33rd minute when Tim Krul's long punt forward was flicked on by Ameobi to Ba, who hooked a stunning volley over Rio Ferdinand's shoulder and into the far corner of the net, his 15th of the season. Not content with just one, the Toon went in search of a second and Ryan Taylor went closest a couple of minutes before the break, curling a free-kick narrowly over after Ba had been felled by Ryan Giggs. Any fears that Newcastle's momentum would be halted by the half-time whistle were swiftly put to bed

two minutes after the restart. Ba was hauled down 25 yards from goal and Cabaye duly stepped up to curl a screamer into the top left-hand corner. And, if it was ever in doubt, the result was put out of sight in the final minute. Krul pumped a free-kick forward and Jones got into a terrible mess with Lindegaard, stooping to head past his own keeper to compound Manchester United's misery.

A delighted Alan Pardew later said: *"We just felt that we had a nice mixture to our game tonight. We put it in the box and were aggressive and we got the reward for that, but we also played some really decent stuff. We were brave at times tonight. We pushed on to them.*

"In the second half, it was important that we didn't sit off Manchester United. We did for about a five-minute spell and they had a couple of good chances. Other than that, we stayed on top of them and never let them play.

"We were aggressive all night and with that, we got a great victory.

"The players deserve a lot of plaudits tonight because they have put in some fantastic performances. You could highlight one or two that were exceptional, but as the team manager, I am just proud of all of them."

Whilst scorer of the second goal Yohan Cabaye added: "It was one of my best free-kicks.

"I used to score a few in France, and I practice them a lot in training, but in a game is totally different.

"When I saw the ball in the goal I was so happy for the team, for the whole of Newcastle, and it was an important goal.

"It was important, not just for me, but for the team as well because it was the second goal and just at the start of the second half.

"It is a very, very good result for us and a brilliant start to the new year. For me, it is the best game and the best win since I have been at Newcastle. I was very happy to be on the pitch tonight."

UNITED: Krul, Simpson, Williamson, Coloccini, Santon, R.Taylor, Cabaye (Perch 78), Tioté, Gutiérrez, Ba (Obertan 90), Shola Ameobi (Best 75).

GOALS: Newcastle - Ba 33, Cabaye 47, Jones Og 90
ATTENDANCE: 52,299

MAY 2ND 2012
PREMIER LEAGUE
CHELSEA 0 NEWCASTLE UNITED 2

Papiss Cissé lit up West London with one of the goals of the season to register United's eighth away win of the season and keep the pressure on the top four in the process. The Senegalese hot-shot had put the visitors in front with an expertly taken volley after 19 minutes. The goal owed much to an impressive run by Davide Santon. The Italian delivered into the feet of Cissé on the edge of the box, and he flicked the ball up before hitting an unstoppable

volley into the top corner. And his fellow forward Demba Ba almost got in on the act as well, forcing a fine, finger-tip save from Čech before smashing a shot against the crossbar from a corner routine which was straight off the training ground. But nothing could prepare Stamford Bridge for what the number nine had up his sleeve in stoppage time. The board had indicated a minimum of ten minutes injury time after a lengthy hold up following an injury to

Cheick Tioté, and with the home side pushing for an equaliser, it looked set to be a nervy finale for Newcastle. Cissé, however, had other ideas. Substitute Ryan Taylor's throw-in down the left was chested into his path by Shola Ameobi before the Toon forward let the ball bounce before striking an incredible long-range effort which swerved from right to left, flying over the head of Petr Čech and into the far corner. The goal sent the travelling fans into raptures and also drew applause from sections of the home fans, and it is being talked about as one of the greatest strikes in Newcastle United's history. It took Cissé's tally in the black and white stripes to an astonishing 13 goals in just 12 appearances, with the result putting the Magpies four points clear of Chelsea in the table – they were eventually to finish one point ahead of the Londoners.

For Alan Pardew, it was his first victory at Chelsea in a lengthy playing and managerial career, and he was delighted with the result: "I'm immensely proud of the players tonight because Wigan (losing 4–0 four days earlier) was such a big disappointment to us all.

"We had a discussion about it, we sorted a few things out, changed our shape and the two strikers had to come and work as midfield players as well as being strikers.

"Their work-rate was phenomenal, but the goals - they change games. His first one was special, the second one was even better.

"There's nothing you can do about that. As soon as he hit it Petr Čech was struggling and it nestled in the far corner.

"For the fans who paid their money to come here, it will live long in their memories, and we will look forward to the highlights DVD because we've had some great goals this season.

"I've been here many, many times as a professional and never won. I'm absolutely delighted with it - it's my result of the season."

UNITED: Krul, Perch, Santon, Williamson, Coloccini, Tioté (R.Taylor 63), Gutiérrez, Ben Arfa (Obertan 87), Cabaye, Ba (Sh.Ameobi 74), Cissé.

GOALS: Newcastle - Cissé 19, 90+4
ATTENDANCE: 41,559

Midfield

The midfielder is a key role in any team, creating chances but also being able to support the defence when necessary. Stamina, vision and a great footballing brain are just three of the qualities needed to play this crucial role and here, not including any of the current players, we've lined up ten of the best over recent years on Tyneside

Paul Gascoigne
(1985-1988)

An FA Youth Cup winner with United in 1985, Gascoigne would go on to become one of the outstanding talents of the game. As a teenager he possessed an array of skills and flair that rapidly had the whole country taking notice. With superb vision, passing, shooting and dribbling skills to compliment work rate and a huge passion for the game, he was the best of his generation. Did great things with England too, notably in the 1990 World Cup but after moving to Tottenham and injuring his knee in the 1991 FA Cup Final, he was, sadly, never quite the same player again.

David Ginola
(1995-1997)

An outstanding talent, David joined Kevin Keegan's side from Paris St Germain. A virtuoso of the highest quality, he had immaculate balance and poise, was two-footed and in his first season on Tyneside, delivered the goods with entertainment to boot. Able to bamboozle every defender in the land, Ginola's wing play was exceptional. A pin-up star too, Ginola was a rare talent who thrilled supporters on both sides of the Channel. Sadly he never really made his mark with the French National Team.

Peter Beardsley
(1983-1987 & 1993-1997)

A true United legend, Peter appeared for the Magpies in two separate spells, first with the likes of Kevin Keegan and Chris Waddle in the mid 1980s, and then under Keegan the Manager, 10 years on when the Magpies took the Premiership by storm. Peter is recognised by many as the best player to have pulled on the black and white shirt, slight of build but possessing fantastic ball skills and marvellous vision. The holder of 59 England caps, Peter scored 119 goals in 326 appearances for United, many of which were truly spectacular – the end product of splendid placement, precision timing or delightful dribbles.

Maestros

Terry Hibbitt
(1971-1975 & 1978-1981)

Brought to St. James' Park by Joe Harvey, Terry was one of United's best-ever bargain buys. Although small and frail-looking, he possessed a sweet left foot and forged a great understanding from his midfield role, in tandem with Tony Green, with the likes of Malcolm Macdonald and John Tudor up front. A superb ball player, with a terrific range of passing, Terry is sadly no longer with us but is perhaps best remembered by supporters for his masterful display in the 1974 FA Cup semi-final win against Burnley.

Robert Lee
(1992-2002)

One of the best all-round midfielders in the Premiership, Rob moved to Gallowgate from Charlton where he had made over 300 appearances. Strong in possession, full of energy, and an accomplished goalscorer, he made the central midfield role his own whilst becoming a regular member of the England set-up, scoring on his debut. Lee became the first United player to net a European hat-trick, the first coming after only 50 seconds in Antwerp, the quickest of all United's 208 European goals.

Terry McDermott
(1973-1974 & 1982-1984)

Terry McDermott enjoyed two very successful spells as a player on Tyneside. He began his playing career with Bury before Joe Harvey brought him to St. James' Park in January 1973. A midfielder with great vision, skill and stamina, Terry moved to Liverpool in 1974 where he enjoyed huge success before Arthur Cox brought him back to Gallowgate in 1982. Terry teamed up with Kevin Keegan, Chris Waddle and Peter Beardsley to lead the club back to Division One in 1984. An England regular too, Terry also served United well as a coach.

Tony Green (1971-1973)

Although only making 39 appearances for the Magpies, the all too brief Newcastle United career of Tony Green is fondly cherished by all those supporters fortunate enough to have seen him play. Brought to Tyneside by Joe Harvey from Blackpool, Tony had exceptional ability on the ball and buzzing with enthusiasm, he would dart into action jinking past players in midfield. Also possessing a thundering shot and a stunning change of pace, his career was tragically cut short when a knee ligament injury forced his retirement from the game. Green was a genius in every sense of the word and who knows what else he could have gone on to achieve in the game.

Midfield Maestros

Jimmy Smith
(1969-1976)

'Jinky' Jimmy Smith was an outstanding ball player who was United's first 'six-figure' incoming transfer when he moved from Aberdeen. A master craftsman, 'Jinky' could send the crowd into raptures when 'in the mood'. He had a languid, lazy style and possessed a tantalising right foot. Hampered by knee injuries, he was good enough to win International honours for Scotland. His magical performances mean he will always be remembered as one of United's finest.

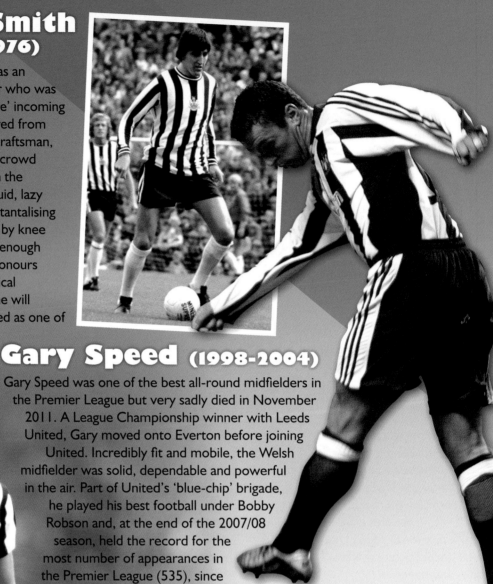

Gary Speed (1998-2004)

Gary Speed was one of the best all-round midfielders in the Premier League but very sadly died in November 2011. A League Championship winner with Leeds United, Gary moved onto Everton before joining United. Incredibly fit and mobile, the Welsh midfielder was solid, dependable and powerful in the air. Part of United's 'blue-chip' brigade, he played his best football under Bobby Robson and, at the end of the 2007/08 season, held the record for the most number of appearances in the Premier League (535), since overtaken by Ryan Giggs.

Chris Waddle (1980-1985)

Chris Waddle was an immensely talented ball playing winger who helped set United alight in the early to mid 1980s. Having signed from non-league Tow Law, Chris had a slow start at St. James' Park but blossomed into an international class talent, mainly under the astute guidance of manager Arthur Cox. With the rare ability to go past defenders using a body swerve and deceptive pace, Waddle played right across United's front line putting in dangerous crosses or hitting the target with viciously bending shots. Chris won 62 England caps and played in the 1986 and 1990 World Cups and is perhaps most 'famous' for missing the vital penalty against West Germany in the semi finals of Italia '90.

QUIZZES

QUIZ no. 1

What do you remember about the 2011/12 season?

1. Who scored United's last goal of 2011?

2. Who knocked United out of the FA Cup?

3. Who scored United's first hat-trick of the season?

4. Which team did United sign Yohan Cabaye from?

5. Who saw the first red card in a United fixture last season?

6. Which three teams did Newcastle fail to beat last season?

7. Which three teams did United do the 'double' over last season?

8. Which two players did Tim Krul save penalties from?

9. After scoring in six successive games, which team prevented Papiss Cissé making it seven?

10. Against which team did United record their highest home attendance in 2011/12?

QUIZ no. 2

See how much you know about Newcastle United past and present

1. In which year did Newcastle United play at the Millennium Stadium?

2. Who was Newcastle's first Premier League game against in 1993?

3. Paul Goddard, Demba Ba and Pop Robson all have connections with which other team?

4. Who did United beat when they won the FA Cup for the last time in 1955?

5. Who were United's first ever European opponents in 1968?

6. Club legend Bobby Moncur captained which National team?

7. Which country did midfielder Clarence Acuna play for?

8. Which German team did Papiss Cissé play for?

9. United's worst Premier League defeat was 6–0 against which team?

10. Who is the only German to play for United in the Premier League?

Answers on P62

FA Cup/League Cup Reviews

ROVERS END CARLING CUP DREAM
Rd 2: SCUNTHORPE 1 – 2 NEWCASTLE UNITED
Rd 3: NOTTM FOREST 3 – 4 NEWCASTLE UNITED
Rd 4: BLACKBURN ROVERS 4 – 3 NEWCASTLE UNITED

United's record in the League Cup is, to put it mildly, not the best. One solitary Final appearance (back in 1976) in the 50-year history of the competition isn't a lot to crow about – sadly 2011/12 was to be no different, even though hopes were high, as always on Tyneside when the word 'Cup' is mentioned.

The road to Wembley began at Glanford Park, home of Scunthorpe United. In front of a live TV audience, sensing an upset no doubt, United were in danger of falling at the first hurdle. Chris

Dagnall put The Iron one up after 15 minutes and it wasn't until 10 minutes before the end that Ryan Taylor netted a superb dead ball equaliser. The Magpies were indebted to Sammy Ameobi whose first goal for the club earned United an extra time victory.

The Magpies were on the road again in Round Three, this time to struggling Championship outfit Nottingham Forest and in a belter of a game, seven goals were shared between the two clubs with United's winner coming courtesy of a 120th

minute header from captain Fabricio Coloccini which spared both sides the somewhat fearsome prospect of a penalty shoot-out.

The 'draw gods' weren't on United's side once again as a third successive away tie awaited Newcastle in Round Four, this time at Ewood Park. And as the clock ticked over 90 minutes it looked like curtains for a United side trailing by 2-0. But then out of the blue, Danny Guthrie rifled in a 20-yard cracker in the third minute of injury time and in the final minute of the six

extra minutes played, a stunning Yohan Cabaye free-kick amazingly sent the tie into extra time, stunning the home regulars in the stadium.

It wasn't to be though for United, going into the extra 30 minutes in the ascendancy didn't help the visitors as it was their turn to suffer last minute agony as Gaël Givet rose unchallenged at the back post to head Rovers into the quarter finals of the competition. For United it was their first defeat of the season after a very commendable 11-game unbeaten run.

ALBION PROVE THORN IN UNITED SIDE ONCE AGAIN
Rd 3: NEWCASTLE UNITED 2 – 1 BLACKBURN ROVERS
Rd 4: BRIGHTON 1 – 0 NEWCASTLE UNITED

The FA Cup remains a magical competition, no more so than for fans of Newcastle United, and once again, come the first week of January, hopes were high that this was to be 'our' year.

A first home cup-tie of the season against Blackburn Rovers looked to be an eminently winnable match and so it proved, but only after a last gasp winner – a recurring feature in United's cup games this particular season.

David Goodwillie gave the visitors a half time lead and with time running out and United looking short of ideas, it took a goal in a million from Hatem Ben Arfa to bring Newcastle level. A goal Alan Pardew described as probably the greatest he had ever witnessed, saw the Frenchman pick the ball up on the right-hand side of the pitch before dribbling past five or six helpless defenders with amazing skill before powering a left foot shot past the helpless Mark Bunn.

A long trip to the south coast was United's reward for putting Rovers out of the competition and it gave Newcastle an opportunity to avenge two FA Cup defeats to the Seagulls, suffered back in the 1980s.

But a low key United performance left their travelling fans frustrated and a single Will Buckley strike 15 minutes from time, which was deflected past Tim Krul by Mike Williamson, was enough to send the AMEX Stadium regulars home with huge smiles on their faces.

United were left to lick their wounds and move on, which is exactly what they did, by travelling to Ewood Park and coming away with three valuable points.

Derby Encounters

The Newcastle United – Sunderland rivalry is one of the most fierce in football and thankfully, for United fans anyway, in recent years the Geordies hold the upper hand in terms of walking away from games with beaming smiles. The fixture last March, which saw Shola Ameobi score an injury time equaliser, was the 134th Tyne-Wear league derby and the 146th match in total between the two sides. In the last 45 years, of the 40 league games played, Newcastle have won 17, 18 have been drawn with Sunderland winning just 5. United have won 8 of the last 13 and have never failed to score against Sunderland in the Premier League whilst Sunderland have drawn a blank on five occasions.

RECENT ENCOUNTERS

Season	Match Number	Home	Score		Away
1967/68	95	Newcastle	2	1	Sunderland
	96	Sunderland	3	3	Newcastle
1968/69	97	Sunderland	1	1	Newcastle
	98	Newcastle	1	1	Sunderland
1969/70	99	Newcastle	3	0	Sunderland
	100	Sunderland	1	1	Newcastle
1976/77	101	Newcastle	2	0	Sunderland
	102	Sunderland	2	2	Newcastle
1978/79	103	Sunderland	1	1	Newcastle
	104	Newcastle	1	4	Sunderland
1979/80	105	Newcastle	3	1	Sunderland
	106	Sunderland	1	0	Newcastle
1984/85	107	Newcastle	3	1	Sunderland
	108	Sunderland	0	0	Newcastle
1989/90	109	Sunderland	0	0	Newcastle
	110	Newcastle	1	1	Sunderland
1991/92	111	Sunderland	1	1	Newcastle
	112	Newcastle	1	0	Sunderland
1992/93	113	Sunderland	1	2	Newcastle
	114	Newcastle	1	0	Sunderland
1996/97	115	Sunderland	1	2	Newcastle
	116	Newcastle	1	1	Sunderland
1999/00	117	Newcastle	1	2	Sunderland
	118	Sunderland	2	2	Newcastle
2000/01	119	Newcastle	1	2	Sunderland
	120	Sunderland	1	1	Newcastle
2001/02	121	Newcastle	1	1	Sunderland
	122	Sunderland	0	1	Newcastle
2002/03	123	Newcastle	2	0	Sunderland
	124	Sunderland	0	1	Newcastle
2005/06	125	Newcastle	3	2	Sunderland
	126	Sunderland	1	4	Newcastle
2007/08	127	Sunderland	1	1	Newcastle
	128	Newcastle	2	0	Sunderland
2008/09	129	Sunderland	2	1	Newcastle
	130	Newcastle	1	1	Sunderland
2010/11	131	Newcastle	5	1	Sunderland
	132	Sunderland	1	1	Newcastle
2011/12	133	Sunderland	0	1	Newcastle
	134	Newcastle	1	1	Sunderland

	Total Record	League Record	FA Cup Record	League Cup Record	Play Offs Record
Played	146	134	8	2	2
Newcastle win	53	51	2	0	0
Sunderland win	46	41	3	1 (on pens)	1
Draws	47	42	3	1	1
For	220	208	8	4	0
Against	213	196	11	4	2

Longest unbeaten sequence (Lge)		Longest winning sequence (Lge)		League Doubles	
Newcastle	9 matches (1967–79, 2001–08)	Newcastle	5 matches (2002–06)	Newcastle	8
Sunderland	7 matches (1957–63)	Sunderland	3 matches (1923–24)	Sunderland	5

Derby Encounters

GOALSCORERS AGAINST SUNDERLAND IN LEAGUE FOOTBALL, 1898 - 2012			
Eleven	**Seven**	**Six**	**Five**
Jackie Milburn (in 15 games)	Shola Ameobi	Albert Shepherd Own Goals	George Robledo

Four	**Three**	**Two**
Jackie Rutherford, William Hibbert, Stan Seymour, Neil Harris, Tom McDonald, Tommy Lang, Bobby Mitchell, Vic Keeble, Alex Tait, Peter Beardsley, Kevin Nolan	Ronald Orr, Jimmy Howie, Tom Urwin, Hughie Gallacher, Jimmy Boyd, Reg Davies, Tom Curry, Len White, Alan Shearer	Jock Peddie, Alex Gardner, Colin Veitch, George Wilson, Sandy Higgins, James Stewart, Andy Smailes, Harry Bedford, Sam Weaver, Alan Suddick, Wyn Davies, Ollie Burton, Keith Dyson, Paul Cannell, Liam O'Brien, Craig Bellamy, Michael Owen

One

Willie Wardrope, Alex McFarland, John Fraser, Bob McColl, Peter McWilliam, Bill Appleyard, John Scott, Bill McCracken, Andrew Anderson, Thomas Lowes, Tom Hall, John King, Tommy Goodwill, Frank Hudspeth, Ray Robinson, Ted Ward, Robert McIntosh, William Aitken, Bob Clark, William Cowan, Tom Mordue, Bob McKay, Roddy MacKenzie, Duncan Hutchison, Harry McMenemy, JR Richardson, Jack Allen, George Hair, Frank Houghton, Ernie Taylor, Tommy Walker, Joe Harvey, Tommy Casey, Billy Foulkes, Ivor Broadis, John McGuigan, Jimmy Kerray, Colin Taylor, Ron McGarry, Albert Bennett, John McNamee, Pop Robson, Jackie Sinclair, Jimmy Smith, Alan Kennedy, Tommy Craig, John Connolly, Peter Withe, Peter Cartwright, Tommy Cassidy, Alan Shoulder, Mark McGhee, David Kelly, Scott Sellars, Les Ferdinand, Kieron Dyer, Didier Domi, Helder, Gary Speed, Andy O'Brien, Nikos Dabizas, Nobby Solano, Emre, Michael Chopra, Charles N'Zogbia, Albert Luque, James Milner, Ryan Taylor

HAT TRICK HEROES

Alex Tait, 22 December 1956,
(Newcastle 6 – 2 Sunderland)

Peter Beardsley, 1 January 1985,
(Newcastle 3 – 1 Sunderland)

Kevin Nolan, 31 October 2010,
(Newcastle 5 – 1 Sunderland)

FIRST GOALSCORER

Willie Wardrope, 24 December 1898,
(Sunderland 2 – 3 Newcastle)

LAST GOALSCORER

Shola Ameobi, 4 March 2012,
(Newcastle 1 – 1 Sunderland

OVER 50 GOALS FOR UNITED,
BUT NONE V SUNDERLAND

Malcolm Macdonald (95), Jack Smith (69),
Mick Quinn (59), Andy Cole (55),
John Tudor (53), Billy Cairns (51)
* Macdonald, Tudor and Cole never
played against them

THEIR ONLY UNITED LEAGUE GOAL
WAS AGAINST SUNDERLAND

John Scott (1911/12)
Albert Luque (2005/06)

CUP GOALS

FA CUP (8)
Albert Shepherd (2), George Wilson
(2), Ronald Orr, Jackie Rutherford,
Colin Veitch, John McTavish

LEAGUE CUP (4)
Ian Davies, Peter Cartwright,
Stuart Boam, Alan Shoulder

Player Profiles

MEHDI ABEID

Born: 6 August 1992, Montreuil, France
Debut: 20 September 2011 v Nottm Forest (A)
Previous Club: Lens, Appearances/Goals: 2/0

Mehdi arrived on Tyneside from Lens on 1 July 2011 signing a five-year deal after a successful trial at the end of the 2010/11 season. He has represented France at Under-17 and Under-18 level and is a right footed attacking midfielder who can also play in a forward position. Of French/Algerian descent he impressed when given his chance, notably in the Carling Cup and will be looking to 2012/13 to make his mark on Tyneside where the battle for midfield places is particularly intense.

ROMAIN AMALFITANO

Born: 27 August 1989, Nice
Debut: 13 July 2012 v Chemnitzer FC (A)
Previous Club: Reims, Appearances/Goals: 0/0

Born in Nice, Amalfitano is a versatile midfielder who is equally comfortable operating on either the right flank or in a central role. He came through the youth system at Châteauroux before starting his senior career with Evian. From there, Amalfitano joined Reims in 2010, and played at the Stade Auguste Delaune for the last two seasons, helping them achieve promotion back to League 1 last season. Amalfitano has an older brother, Morgan, who plays for Marseille.

SAMMY AMEOBI

Born: 1 May 1992, Newcastle
Debut: 15 May 2011 v Chelsea (A)
Previous Club: Academy, Appearances/Goals: 14/1

The third Ameobi to join the Club after brothers Shola and Tomi. From Grindon Hall School, he represented Newcastle Schoolboys before making his Reserve team debut in September 2008. Sammy made his bow for Nigeria's U20 side in March 2011 in a friendly fixture staged in Dubai, against Egypt. He then made his Premier League debut as a substitute at Chelsea on 15 May 2011, with brother Shola on the pitch too. Scored his first senior goal for United, the extra time winner, in the 2–1 Carling Cup win at Scunthorpe in August 2011.

SHOLA AMEOBI

Born: 12 October 1981, Zaria, Nigeria
Debut: 9 September 2000 v Chelsea (H)
Previous Club: Academy, Appearances/Goals: 333/72

Scorer of some very important goals last season, notably against Tottenham and Sunderland - his seventh strike against United's deadliest rivals. A talented striker with a penchant for the unpredictable, Shola was born in Nigeria and came to England with his parents at the age of five. A product of the Academy, he is United's second all-time leading European scorer with 12 goals. Shola, hugely respected at the club, has passed the 300-game mark for the Magpies and with 72 United goals to his name, should have a key role to play once more in 2012/13.

VURNON ANITA

Born: 4 April 1989, Netherlands Antilles
Debut: 18 August 2012 v Tottenham (H)
Previous Club: Ajax, Appearances/Goals: 0/0

The Holland international defender, who is equally at home in midfield joined Newcastle United in August 2012, signing a five-year contract. Vernon was born in Willemstad in the Netherlands Antilles (in the Caribbean) and moved to Holland with his family in 1997 where he joined local side VV Maarssen. He began his association with Ajax in 1999 and made his senior club debut in 2006. Capped for the first time in 2010 against Mexico, he now has three full caps having previously played at U17, U19 and U21 level. Won the Eredivisie with Ajax last season.

DEMBA BA

Born: 25 May 1985, Paris
Debut: 13 August 2011 v Arsenal (H)
Previous Club: West Ham, Appearances/Goals: 36/16

Senegal international striker Demba Ba joined Newcastle United in June 2011, signing a three-year contract. The former West Ham front man, who scored 7 goals in 13 appearances for the Hammers in 2010/11, hit the ground running last season hitting 16 goals and finishing as United's top scorer. One of eight children, and many fans' signing of the season, he has been capped 15 times by Senegal, with three international goals to his name. Ba has also had spells with Rouen, Mouscron and 1899 Hoffenheim.

HATEM BEN ARFA

Born: 7 March 1987, Paris
Debut: 11 September 2010 v Blackpool (H)
Previous Club: Marseille, Appearances/Goals: 34/7

Ben Arfa came to prominence at France's Clairefontaine youth academy Hatem joined Marseille in 2008 after winning his first full international cap against the Faroe Islands, when he netted the first of two goals to date. Scored a cracker, and United's winner, on his full debut at Everton in September 2010 but suffered a double leg break at Manchester City in October 2010 keeping him sidelined for the rest of the season. Excelled during 2011/12 and also scored two of the most breath-taking goals seen on Tyneside. Represented France at Euro 2012.

GAEL BIGIRIMANA

Born: 22 October 1993, Burundi
Debut: 23 August 2012 v Atromitos (A)
Previous Club: Coventry City
Appearances/Goals: 0/0

The Burundi born 18-year-old midfielder joined United on 6 July from Coventry City, signing a five-year contract after the Magpies agreed an undisclosed fee with the Sky Blues. Bigirimana played 26 times in the Championship in 2011/12 and won the Division's Apprentice of the Year award. He had been with Coventry since 2004 and is expected to link up with Willie Donachie and Peter Beardsley's Development Squad at the beginning of his Tyneside career.

YOHAN CABAYE

Born: 14 January 1986, Tourcoing, France
Debut: 13 August 2011 v Arsenal (H)
Previous Club: Lille, Appearances/Goals: 38/5

Cabaye played a key role in Lille clinching their first double since the 1945/46 season and Cabaye's maiden domestic honours before moving to England in June 2011. Creative and an excellent passer, Yohan, a virtual ever-present, had a very impressive first season in the Premier League, creating and scoring a number of superb goals. Brilliant with dead ball kicks too, Yohan adds to the list of outstanding French talent that has served United well in the past. Represented France at Euro 2012

PAPISS CISSÉ

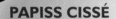

Born: 3 June 1985, Dakar
Debut: 5 February 2012 v Aston Villa (H)
Previous Club: Freiburg, Appearances/Goals: 14/13

Papiss joined United from SC Freiburg and was handed the iconic number 9 shirt at United. He began his career with AS Douanes, in Dakar, and went on to have prolific spells at French clubs Metz, Cherbourg and Châteauroux. In December 2009, he switched to German outfit SC Freiburg, where he struck 37 goals in just 65 appearances. Began his United career with a bang hitting a spectacular winner against Aston Villa. Hit 13 goals, many spectacular, in his first 14 games in the Premier League, scoring in six consecutive games.

FABRICIO COLOCCINI

Born: 22 January 1982, Córdoba
Debut: 17 August 2008 v Man Utd (A)
Previous Club: Deportivo La Coruña
Appearances/Goals: 154/5

An outstanding performer last season where his leadership and calm authority as captain did much to earn United fifth place. Fabricio joined United from Deportivo La Coruña in 2008 and after taking time to settle and adapt, is now one of the most recognisable faces in the Premier League. He began his career with Argentinos Juniors and made his professional debut in 1998 with Boca Juniors before moving to AC Milan. In 2004 he was an Olympic Gold medallist and he also played in the 2006 World Cup in Germany.

ROB ELLIOT

Born: 30 April 1986, London
Debut: 20 September 2011 v Nottingham Forest (A)
Previous Club: Charlton, Appearances/Goals: 1/0

Joined United in August 2011 signing a five-year deal. Rob signed a professional deal with the Addicks in 2004, and made 109 appearances for the south-east London side, with a number of those coming during Alan Pardew's time at The Valley. He has also spent time on loan at Bishop's Stortford, Notts County and Accrington Stanley. Made his United bow in the Carling Cup at Nottingham Forest but spent most of the season as back up to Tim Krul.

SHANE FERGUSON

Born: 12 July 1991, Derry, Northern Ireland
Debut: 25 August 2010 v Accrington (A)
Previous Club: Academy
Appearances/Goals: 18/0

From Derry in Northern Ireland, Shane, skilful and strong, despite his small stature, played his early football at Maiden City. He made his Northern Ireland U21 debut in 2008 against Scotland and won his first full cap coming on as a substitute in Pisa versus Italy on 6 June 2009 (age 17 yrs 329 days). After featuring in the 2010/11 pre-season games, Shane made his full United debut in the League Cup tie at Accrington on 25 August 2010. Suffered from injury in 2011/12 but hopeful of staking his claims further in 2012/13.

CURTIS GOOD

Born: 13 March 1993, Melbourne, Australia
Debut:
Previous Club: Melbourne Heart
Appearances/Goals: 0/0

Born in Melbourne, Australia, Curtis began his career with Box Hill United and Nunawading City in Melbourne before moving to the Australian Institute of Sport. Captaining the AIS, he then joined Melbourne Heart in the Australian A League in 2011. Signing a six-year deal at United, Curtis, primarily a centre half, made 25 appearances for Heart last season in his first full professional season. Has represented Australia three times at Under-20 level

DAN GOSLING

Born: 1 February 1990, Brixham, Devon
Debut: 16 January 2011 v Sunderland (A)
Previous Club: Everton
Appearances/Goals: 14/1

Dan moved to United from Everton in July 2010 signing a four-year contract. The Brixham (Devon) born midfielder had moved to Everton from Plymouth in the January 2008 transfer window having made his debut for the Pilgrims aged just 16. Remembered by Evertonians for his 118th-minute winner in an FA Cup fourth round replay against rivals Liverpool which truly brought his name to the fore. 2010/11 was a struggle for Dan as he spent much of it on the sidelines recovering from a cruciate knee ligament injury. Back to full fitness and looking to impress once again.

JONÁS GUTIÉRREZ

Born: 5 July 1983, Buenos Aires, Argentina
Debut: 17 August 2008 v Man Utd (A)
Previous Club: Vélez Sársfield
Appearances/Goals: 153/10

Argentina International Jonás Gutiérrez enjoyed a terrific 2011/12 campaign with many outstanding displays down the United flanks. After a barren 2008/09 season in front of goal, his nickname of Spiderman, for wearing the superhero's webbed mask during flamboyant goal celebrations, has lit up Tyneside in the past three seasons. Previously with Velez Sarsfield in Argentina and Mallorca, Spain, his endeavour and enterprise have brought him many admirers. United's only representative at the 2010 World Cup, he missed only one game in United's 2011/12 Premier League campaign.

STEVE HARPER

Born: 14 March 1975, Easington
Debut: 28 November 1998 v Wimbledon (H)
Previous Club: Seaham Red Star
Appearances/Goals: 190/0

An integral part of United's success in 2009/10 when he kept a club record 21 clean sheets as United stormed to the Championship title. Very popular on and off the pitch at St. James' Park the Easington-born shot-stopper is one of the top English goalkeepers in the country. He initially broke into the first team during the 1998/99 season and then played in the 1999 FA Cup Final against Manchester United. Possesses terrific reflexes and is a commanding presence in the 18-yard box. Lost out to Tim Krul in the number one stakes last season but just the man you need in a crisis or if called upon.

TIM KRUL

Born: 3 April 1988, The Hague, Holland
Debut: 2 November 2006 v Palmero (A)
Previous Club: Den Haag
Appearances/Goals: 76/0

An ever-present last season and enjoyed a fabulous campaign to boot with a string of outstanding saves. Tim joined United from Dutch side Den Haag in July 2005 and made his debut in the UEFA Cup against Palmero in Sicily in November 2006, turning in a man of the match performance. His league debut came at the Hawthorns on the opening day of the 2009/10 campaign when he replaced the injured Steve Harper. In 2011/12 he made 21 first team appearances and topped that off by making his full international debut against Brazil in June, keeping a clean sheet.

SYLVAIN MARVEAUX

Born: 15 April 1986, Vannes, France
Debut: 25 August 2011 v Scunthorpe (A)
Previous Club: Rennes
Appearances/Goals: 10/0

Sylvain Marveaux was born in Vannes in the Brittany region of France and joined local club AS Ménimur at the age of six. He then joined Vannes OC whilst attending the Pôle Espoirs Football de Ploufragan, a regional version of the Clairefontaine Academy. He made his Rennes debut in the 2006/07 season when he also earned 11 caps for the France Under-21 team, scoring four goals. Brother Joris plays in the French Ligue 1 for Montpellier. Last season was hampered by serious injury so 2012/13 looks to be an important season for the likeable Frenchman.

GABRIEL OBERTAN

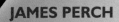

Born: 26 February 1989, Pantin, France
Debut: 13 August 2011 v Arsenal (H)
Previous Club: Manchester United
Appearances/Goals: 26/1

Gabriel joined the Magpies in August 2011 from Manchester United. A former attendee of the famous Clairefontaine Academy, Obertan began his professional career playing for Bordeaux in France, before joining Manchester United in July 2009. Gaby has represented his country at Under-16, Under-17, Under-18, Under-19 and Under-21 level but is still to earn his senior debut. Scored his first Premier League goal at Blackburn on 1 February 2012.

JAMES PERCH

Born: 28 September 1985, Mansfield
Debut: 16 August 2010 v Manchester United (A)
Previous Club: Nottingham Forest, **Appearances/Goals:** 43/0

James, nicknamed 'Perchinho' by the Toon Army, signed for United from Nottingham Forest in July 2010 after scoring 12 goals in 220 games for the Reds after making his debut as an 18-year-old in 2004. He joined Forest's Academy in 2003 and has shown his versatility by playing across the back-four and in midfield. Last season, his first in the Premier League, he made 15 appearances but was hindered by injuries and some unfortunate yellow cards. 2011/12 showed what he could do as he produced countless solid reliable and outstanding displays.

DAVIDE SANTON

Born: 2 January 1991, Portomaggiore, Ferrara, Italy
Debut: 16 October 2011 v Tottenham (H)
Previous Club: Inter Milan, **Appearances/Goals:** 27/0

Arrived from Inter Milan in August 2011, the 21-year-old is a left-back who can also play on the right-hand side, as well as in an advanced position. He joined Inter's youth set-up at the age of 14 from Ravenna, and was originally a winger before being moved back into a defensive role. Davide made his international debut for Italy against Northern Ireland in Pisa in June 2009 - the same game in which Magpies youngster Shane Ferguson also made his international bow. In 2009, former Italy head coach Marcello Lippi described Santon as reminding him of "a young Paolo Maldini."

DANNY SIMPSON

Born: 4 January 1987, Manchester
Debut: 19 August 2009 v Sheffield Wednesday (A)
Previous Club: Manchester United, Appearances/Goals: 112/2

Joined the Magpies on loan in August 2009 from Manchester United, the deal becoming permanent in January 2010. Made the right back position his own, making the third most appearances in the league in 2009/10 (39), and for the past two seasons was a virtual ever-present after recovering from a May 2010 ankle operation. Added a second United goal to his name against Nottingham Forest in the Carling Cup, Danny remains a solid, dependable and very popular figure around St. James' Park.

JAMES TAVERNIER

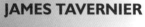

Born: 31 October 1991, Bradford
Debut: 22 September 2009 v Peterborough (A)
Previous Club: Academy, Appearances/Goals: 2/0

Versatile defender able to play full-back or centre-half. Joined United from Walbottle School where he attended from age 15 after moving from West Yorkshire. From 9 years old he played six seasons with Leeds United before moving to Tyneside. Made his 'first team' bow as a substitute in the 1–0 friendly win at Huddersfield on 21 July 2009 and played in the Carling Cup ties at Peterborough and Accrington. Spent time on loan at Sheffield Wednesday and MK Dons last season as he aims to push for first team football on Tyneside in 2012/13.

RYAN TAYLOR

Born: 19 August 1984, Liverpool
Debut: 7 February 2009 v West Brom (A)
Previous Club: Wigan, Appearances/Goals: 87/9

Ryan (over the wall) Taylor signed for United in February 2009 from Wigan as part of the deal that saw Charles N'Zogbia move in the opposite direction. Ryan began his career at Tranmere before a £750,000 move to Wigan in 2005. Able to fill both the full-back berths, Ryan is a hard tackling defender, comfortable on the ball and with bundles of energy. A great ball-striker, he possesses a deadly free-kick which Sunderland will testify to. His versatility serves United well as he proved with a long and successful stint at left back during United's unbeaten start to last season.

STEVEN TAYLOR

Born: 23 January 1986, Greenwich, London
Debut: 25 March 2004 v Real Mallorca (A)
Previous Club: Wycombe (loan), Appearances/Goals: 202/13

Steven, a powerful and dominating centre-half, and with a new contract signed and sealed in 2011, was a solid performer for United last season until injury in December against Chelsea sadly ended his season. A leader in the best Geordie traditions, his passion and will to win for himself, the team, and the supporters is unbridled - witness his three goals in the final three Premier League games of the 2010/11 campaign. Formerly captain of the England Under-21 team, he has also represented England 'B'. Off the field Steven is the perfect ambassador for United.

CHEICK TIOTÉ

Born: 21 June 1986, Yamoussoukro, Ivory Coast
Debut: 18 September 2010 v Everton (A)
Previous Club: FC Twente, Appearances/Goals: 52/1

Outstanding in his two seasons on Tyneside, Cheick began his career with Ivorian side FC Bibo in his native Yamoussoukro, before being picked up by Anderlecht in 2005. Joining FC Twente in July 2008, he won the Dutch title in 2009/10 under the guidance of Steve McClaren. Tioté appeared in all three of the Ivory Coast's group games at the World Cup in South Africa. Scored his first United goal, a stunning left footed 30 yard volley, to make it 4-4 in the dramatic draw with Arsenal at St. James' Park in February 2011 and agreed a new 6½-year contract later that month.

HARIS VUCKIC

Born: 21 August 1992, Ljubljana, Slovenia
Debut: 26 August 2009 v Huddersfield Town (H)
Previous Club: NK Domzale
Appearances/Goals: 12/0

Promising Slovenian born striker who began his career with NK Domzale. Haris has represented Slovenia at U14, U16 and U17 level and was named Player of the Tournament in the Foca Cup in Bosnia in May 2009, scoring five goals in three games. Made his full United debut at Peterborough on 22 September 2009 but injury has held back his progress since then. Called up to the senior Slovenian squad for the Euro 2012 qualifiers in October 2010 he signed new 4½-year contract in January 2011. Showed glimpses of what he can do in 2011/12 and needs more of the same this season.

MIKE WILLIAMSON

Born: 8 November 1983, Stoke
Debut: 27 January 2010 v Crystal Palace (H)
Previous Club: Portsmouth
Appearances/Goals: 73/0

Joined the Magpies in January 2010 from Portsmouth. Stoke born, Williamson started out at Torquay United in 2001 before signing for Southampton. Loan spells back at Torquay, Doncaster and Wycombe followed before a permanent switch to Adams Park in 2005. He joined Watford in 2009 before moving on to Portsmouth. Slotted seamlessly into the United back four for the latter part of the Championship winning campaign and after an excellent debut year in the Premier League, enjoyed a solid 2012 alongside Fabricio Coloccini last season.

Papiss Cissé - 6 of the best

After joining the Magpies in January 2012, Papiss scored some of the most memorable and spectacular goals United fans have ever had the pleasure of seeing. Here we relive six of the best!

Aston Villa

Norwich

Liverpool

Swansea

Stoke

Chelsea

37

Review 2005/06

Graeme Souness began his first full season in charge at St. James' Park and as a prelude to the Premiership kicking off, United were involved in the Intertoto Cup once again. But as happened four seasons earlier, it didn't provide them with a ticket to the UEFA Cup. Victory over the Slovakian side Dubnica landed United with a difficult semi-final against Deportivo La Coruña and it was the Spanish who prevailed, winning both legs 2-1.

An opening-day fixture at Highbury wasn't the ideal start for United and the 2-0 defeat there was the first of four scoreless games for the Magpies before Charles N'Zogbia opened United's account against Fulham after a 438-minute goal famine. That fixture also marked Michael Owen's debut for Newcastle, the prolific England striker having arrived on Tyneside for a record £16m from Real Madrid. And a week later, at Blackburn, the little maestro opened his Newcastle account with the second of United's three goals.

In the domestic cup competitions, a hard-fought victory at Grimsby in the League Cup was followed by a bitterly disappointing loss at Wigan when the hosts fielded a virtual reserve line-up. The FA Cup proved more fruitful with a run to the Quarter Finals before Chelsea put an end to any silverware dreams with a single-goal victory at Stamford Bridge. The Fourth Round tie with Mansfield at St. James' Park was also notable for Alan Shearer equalling Jackie Milburn's Newcastle United goalscoring record of 200 goals.

Consistent league form was proving elusive though and in the run-up to Christmas, the Magpies never rose above 10th place. Then, after three consecutive New Year defeats, the last being a 3-0 drubbing at Manchester City, Souness was sacked and Glenn Roeder, who had been at United's Academy, was asked to take over first-team affairs until the end of the season. The change had an immediate effect as in his first game in charge Portsmouth were beaten 2-0 at St. James' Park – the second goal coming from the boot of Alan Shearer, the record-breaking 201st goal of a quite extraordinary United career. An unbeaten run of four league games followed and although March only brought one win, the last seven games of the season throughout April and May saw the Magpies collect 19 points out of a possible 21 and with it, a very respectable finishing position of 7th. Included in that run was a remarkable 4-1 success on Wearside, notable for four United goals in the last 30 minutes including the last ever from the boot of Alan Shearer, the Geordie hero notching his 206th United goal from the penalty spot before injury brought a premature end to his final season.

Season 2005/06 - Premiership

Pos	Pl	W	D	L	F	A	Pts
7	38	17	7	14	47	42	58

FA Cup: QF

League Cup: R4

UEFA Intertoto:

Top scorer: Shearer 14

Avg Attn: 52,032

Crossword

Answers on P62

Clues Down

1. Jon Dahl from Denmark
2. Welsh striker 1993-95
3. Centre half signed from Rangers
4. Utility man with Brazilian nickname
5. Canadian defender
6. Former Huddersfield boss
7. Shaka from Trinidad
8. Belfast Bar Tender
9. Mercurial French winger

Clues Across

1. Shola or Sammy
2. French defender
3. United's Peruvian master
4. Brazilian signed from Lyon
5. Psycho
6. Ruel the winger
7. Fairs Cup captain
8. Keeper in 1999 Cup Final

United's participation in the FA Cup is best forgotten. A 2-2 draw at St. Andrews in Round 3, in a game the Magpies should really have won, preceded a 5-1 home hammering by the Blues in the replay, United's worst home FA Cup loss since Sheffield United won 5-0 at Gallowgate way back in 1914.

The remaining months of the season were somewhat dull with United hovering around mid-table before a winless last six games of the season condemned the Magpies to a lowly 13th-place finish.

Aston Villa and Liverpool were both sent packing pointless from their visits to Tyneside but, aside from those 'highs', the season merely petered out.

Consequently Roeder had to pay the price and after Blackburn left the North-East with three points at the beginning of May, the former United skipper left the Club and coach Nigel Pearson took over as caretaker manager for the final game of the season at Watford.

Glenn Roeder was at the helm for the start of United's 2006/07 campaign having been appointed as manager on a full-time basis in May 2006. And the season started as early as July 15 with a home Intertoto Cup tie with Lillestrøm SK, the first of a 14-game European campaign which was to end in disappointment following a last 16 defeat against AZ Alkmaar in mid-March.

On the domestic front a home win over Wigan Athletic brought joy to the Geordies on the season's opening day. But, following a subsequent run of one win in 12, the Magpies found themselves languishing in the Premier League drop zone. Summer arrival Antoine Sibierski then fired the only goal against Portsmouth at St. James' Park on November 26 and set United on their way to the first of three maximum hauls as Roeder's men climbed clear of the top-flight trapdoor.

Obafemi Martins and Damien Duff were the gaffer's principle signings, at a combined price of £15m, and the former ended his first season in English football as United's leading scorer, many of his 17 strikes being spectacular finishes followed by a trademark somersault celebration.

Meanwhile, a respectable League Cup run was only ended by League Champions Chelsea at St. James' Park at the Quarter Final stage, the campaign being notable for the first competitive penalty shoot-out success for United after seven previously unsuccessful attempts to win the 12-yard lottery, Watford being the ones to suffer when Steve Harper saved from Jordan Stewart.

Season 2006/07 - Premiership

Pos	Pl	W	D	L	F	A	Pts
13	38	11	10	17	38	47	43

FA Cup:	League Cup:	UEFA Cup:
R3	QF	16

Top scorer: Martins 17

Avg Attn: 50,686

Wordsearch

E	X	S	Q	H	N	A	G	I	W	E	R	T	Y	U	I	D
N	Y	T	I	C	R	E	T	S	E	H	C	N	A	M	A	E
E	C	O	A	L	I	V	E	R	P	O	O	L	G	E	I	T
W	B	K	S	M	A	H	N	E	T	T	O	T	S	I	K	I
C	M	E	D	J	T	Y	W	S	W	T	R	L	H	J	S	N
A	R	S	E	N	A	L	S	G	E	Y	E	R	J	W	S	U
S	D	L	F	K	S	M	D	O	D	H	E	G	A	N	O	R
T	N	K	W	L	T	N	F	K	C	A	F	N	U	O	U	E
L	A	J	E	O	O	B	J	E	D	J	S	G	Y	R	T	T
E	L	H	S	I	N	V	E	I	G	E	V	H	T	W	H	S
D	R	G	T	U	V	C	N	V	A	H	B	J	R	I	A	E
F	E	F	H	Y	I	G	V	E	E	G	N	T	E	C	M	H
G	D	M	A	H	L	U	F	R	T	R	M	R	W	H	P	C
H	N	D	M	T	L	X	C	F	G	D	T	E	D	J	T	N
K	U	S	G	R	A	W	E	S	T	B	R	O	M	H	O	A
J	S	E	E	R	T	Y	U	I	O	T	R	H	N	D	N	M
S	R	E	G	N	A	R	K	R	A	P	S	N	E	E	U	Q

1) Arsenal	11) Queens Park Rangers
2) Aston Villa	12) Reading
3) Chelsea	13) Stoke
4) Everton	14) Southampton
5) Fulham	15) Sunderland
6) Liverpool	16) Swansea
7) Manchester City	17) Tottenham
8) Manchester United	18) West Brom
9) Newcastle	19) West Ham
10) Norwich	20) Wigan

Answers on P62

The Premier League Records

Newcastle United have played in the Premier League for 18 of its 20 seasons. The Magpies missed out in 1992/93, the first season, when they were winning promotion from the old first division and then of course, after relegation in 2009, United bounced straight back the following season. Despite that United hold a respectable eighth place in the all time table, behind the only seven sides who have never been out of the top flight of English football over the past 20 years.

ALL TIME PREMIER LEAGUE RECORDS (1992/93 – 2011/12)

	Club	Pl	W	D	L	F	A	Pts
1	Manchester United	772	500	164	108	1541	660	1653
2	Arsenal	772	416	203	153	1345	718	1449
3	Chelsea	772	401	199	172	1281	741	1402
4	Liverpool	772	380	194	198	1236	753	1336
5	Aston Villa	772	283	240	249	974	924	1089
6	Tottenham Hotspur	772	294	204	274	1071	1021	1086
7	Everton	772	272	218	282	973	978	1034
8	Newcastle United	692	277	186	229	996	885	1017
9	Blackburn Rovers	696	262	184	250	926	905	972
10	Manchester City	580	210	150	220	766	729	780
11	West Ham United	616	201	157	256	723	879	762
12	Leeds United	468	189	125	154	641	573	692
13	Middlesbrough	536	160	156	220	621	741	636
14	Southampton	506	150	136	220	598	741	586
15	Bolton Wanderers	494	149	128	217	574	743	574
16	Fulham	418	130	121	167	480	553	511
17	Sunderland	418	112	104	204	422	605	440
18	Coventry City	354	99	112	143	387	490	409
19	Sheffield Wed	316	101	89	126	409	453	392
20	Wimbledon	316	99	94	123	384	472	391
21	Charlton Athletic	302	91	81	129	340	441	354
22	Leicester City	308	84	90	134	354	456	342
23	Birmingham City	266	74	83	109	272	356	302
24	Wigan	266	75	67	124	270	408	292
25	Portsmouth	266	77	66	122	289	379	290
26	Derby County	266	68	71	127	271	416	275
27	Q. P. R.	202	69	46	87	266	297	253
28	Norwich City	202	63	61	78	255	322	250
29	Nottm Forest	198	60	59	79	229	287	239
30	Ipswich Town	202	57	53	92	219	312	224
31	West Bromwich	228	52	60	116	232	374	216
32	Stoke City	152	47	42	63	154	204	183
33	Crystal Palace	160	37	49	74	160	245	160
34	Wolverhampton W	152	32	40	80	157	281	136

Furthermore there are a number of players with Newcastle connections who make the top ten charts of goals and appearances in the Premier League

Players	Teams	Goals
Alan Shearer	Southampton/Blackburn/Newcastle	260
Andy Cole	Newcastle/Man Utd/Blackburn/Fulham	187
Thierry Henry	Arsenal	174
Robbie Fowler	Liverpool/Leeds/Man City	163
Les Ferdinand	QPR/NUFC/Spurs/W Ham/Leicester/Bolton	149
Frank Lampard	West Ham/Chelsea	149
Teddy Sheringham	Spurs/Man Utd/Spurs/West Ham	146
Michael Owen	Liverpool/Newcastle/Man Utd	144
Wayne Rooney	Everton/Man Utd	134
Jimmy Floyd Hasselbaink	Chelsea/Middlesbrough/Charlton	127

Players	Teams	Appearances
Ryan Giggs	Manchester United	598
David James	Liverpool/Villa/West Ham/Manchester City/Pompey	573
Gary Speed	Leeds/Everton/Newcastle/Bolton	535
Frank Lampard	West Ham/Chelsea	520
Emile Heskey	Leicester/Liverpool/Birmingham/Wigan/Villa	516
Sol Campbell	Tottenham/Arsenal/Pompey/Newcastle	503
Phil Neville	Man Utd/Everton	487
Jamie Carragher	Liverpool	484
Paul Scholes	Manchester United	482
Alan Shearer	Southampton/Blackburn/Newcastle	441

Spot the Difference

There are 10 differences between these pictures. Find out how you did by checking the answers on page 62

Guess the Autographs

See if you can guess the 15 player autographs.

NEWCASTLE UNITED

1

2

3

4

5

6

7

8

9

10

11

12

13

14

15

Answers on pages 62

Newcastle United Foundation

Newcastle United Foundation is the official charity of Newcastle United Football Club.

It aims to use the local passion for football to encourage learning and promote healthy lifestyles that will make a real difference to the lives of children, young people and families in our region.

Whilst the players consolidated their position in the Premier League in 2010/11, the team at Newcastle United Foundation had a fantastic year of activities out in the community. The Foundation continued to provide opportunities for young people to play football through its grassroots coaching and schools skills programmes and in addition has created a range of educational projects to inspire learning and promote healthy lifestyles, reaching over 10,000 individuals.

Here are some pictures of some of the projects from last season.

Jonás Selects Best Kit

Argentina international Jonás Gutiérrez took part in an Enterprise activity where groups of secondary school children were involved in a whole day of fun and challenging activities designed to improve their business skills. At this event they were tasked with designing and marketing a new Newcastle United strip to sell in the club shop, with Jonás selecting the winner.

The Foundation promotes a healthy active lifestyle and encourages local primary school children to be "Match Fit" like their Newcastle United heroes. Danny Simpson and James Perch joined pupils from St. George's Primary in a walking test to measure their resting heart rates.

Danny and James Get Match Fit

Girls Football Gets a Boost

Girls football continues to grow in popularity and thanks to funding from Awards for All last season the Foundation ran a whole programme of fun football clubs in local primary schools. James Perch visited St. Catherine's in Newcastle to kick off.

The Foundation is keen to help all children to play football, regardless of their ability but at the same time help Newcastle United nurture young talent. Over 300 boys are signed up to the Foundation's Advanced Coaching Programme every season, and who better to pass on his skills to them than local lad Sammy Ameobi.

Sammy Supports Foundation Coaching

Family Football With Demba

Demba visited a Foundation Family Learning project at Windy Nook Primary School in Gateshead and was caught by the BBC Match of the Day cameras. Parents and children sign up to the Foundation's five-week Family Football courses which promote learning together, communication and teamwork. At Windy Nook, the families were delighted when Demba dropped in to help them construct a giant bamboo structure as part of a teamwork exercise.

Local schools visit the stadium every week to take part in fun and interactive educational workshops. Each session includes a stadium tour and a lesson in the Learning centre. Pupils from Dunston Riverside Primary were thrilled to be able to quiz Danny Simpson on his pre-match routine in the home changing room.

Pre-Match Danny

Mike Williamson has joined 19 other Premier League players to use the motivational power of football to encourage children to improve their literacy skills. As part of the Premier League Reading Stars programme, Mike, United's Reading Star, helped set literacy challenges and talked about his favourite books sharing his love of reading with school children. This was also done online via the Premier League's website.

Reading Star Willow

Shola launched a new multi-sport initiative designed to get children playing sport more often. The striker joined players from Newcastle Eagles Basketball team at Benfield School in Newcastle to launch Basketball as part of the Foundation's hugely successful Premier League 4 Sport programme.

Aside from these featured events, United's players took part in a whole range of other activities/events on a weekly basis as part of their commitment to support the local community.

Shola Shoots Hoops

Top Ten Goals 2011/12

It was a cracking season for goals once again, especially on Tyneside with United scoring an incredible number of outstanding strikes, so much so they could have held a goal of the season competition themselves – indeed Papiss Cissé's wonderful second goal at Chelsea was voted Goal of the Season by the BBC – ahead of Peter Crouch's stunning volley against Manchester City. It wasn't easy to select only 10, for example Yohan Cabaye and Jonás Gutiérrez are very unfortunate to miss out, but here they are listed in the order they were scored throughout the season. Unlike in 2010/11, where we chose ten different scorers, some players inevitably feature more than once!

RYAN TAYLOR v SUNDERLAND A, 20/8/11

No better time to score or no better opponent to score against. Just past the hour Jonás Gutiérrez was fouled down the United left just outside the box. Cue Ryan Taylor who hit a masterful right-footed free-kick which eluded the flailing arms of Mignolet before nestling in the back of the net. Namesake Steven gleefully followed it in and 'Ryan Taylor over the wall' was born.

SHOLA AMEOBI v TOTTENHAM H, 16/10/11

United were trailing the Londoners with only five minutes left before local lad Shola hit a superbly-executed leveller. Ryan Taylor delightfully played Shola in down the left, he took a touch, then another before a third touch which was a left-foot thunderbolt, striking the ball low and true beyond Friedel into the bottom corner. Absolutely brilliant and celebrated in true Shola style. Spurs were stunned, but it was no more than United deserved.

DEMBA BA v MANCHESTER UNITED H, 4/1/12

The Champions had started well but on 33 minutes Tim Krul's long kick upfield was met by Shola Ameobi, who beat Phil Jones in the air and flicked it on for Demba. He let the ball bounce before arching a stupendous right-footed shot from 12 yards around Rio Ferdinand and beyond a static Anders Lindegaard. Instinctive, intuitive but brilliant too and it set the Magpies, and their delirious fans, on the road to a fantastic 3-0 win.

HATEM BEN ARFA v BLACKBURN ROVERS H, 7/1/12

Many people's goal of the season, but there again... United were heading out of the FA Cup with 20 minutes remaining when Hatem Ben Arfa took possession of the ball on the right-hand side of the pitch, level with the edge of the centre circle. Ten seconds later, and with 14 touches of the ball, he sublimely struck a left-foot shot from just inside the six yard box into the roof of the net. And yes, he incredibly dribbled past half the Rovers team too. Undoubtedly a world class goal.

PAPISS CISSÉ v ASTON VILLA H, 5/2/12

Cissé was making his debut after returning from the Africa Cup of Nations. With the scores tied on 71 minutes Jonás Gutiérrez swung over a cross from the left which evaded Demba Ba and Richard Dunne. Cissé, in the right place at the right time, instantly controlled ball on his chest before hammering a magnificent left-footed drive into the top corner of the Gallowgate goal for a dream start to life in the famous number nine shirt. Villa keeper Shay Given was utterly helpless and it was a sign of things to come for the Senegal striker.

HATEM BEN ARFA v WEST BROM A, 25/3/12

This was the team goal of the season. United were already one up at the Hawthorns when, defending on the edge of their own penalty box, Hatem Ben Arfa broke clear and played a crisp one-two in his own half with Yohan Cabaye. Then, exchanging passes with Papiss Cissé and with the Baggies back four all over the place, Ben Arfa cut inside and curled a left-footed drive beyond Ben Foster into the far corner. A classic breakaway goal of the highest order.

PAPISS CISSÉ v SWANSEA CITY A, 6/4/12

Swansea were pressing for an equaliser when on 69 mins Hatem Ben Arfa played in Yohan Cabaye, who played through a slide rule pass for Papiss Cissé, who had begun to pull away from the Swansea back four. Leaning away but maintaining his balance and awareness, the striker produced a phenomenal right-footed chip finish over a stranded Michel Vorm. The away fans behind the goal thought the ball was sailing over the bar but it dipped just in time for the most sublime and skillful of executions you will ever see.

HATEM BEN ARFA v BOLTON H, 9/4/12

The deadlock at Gallowgate was broken with a goal in a million. On 73 minutes United keeper Tim Krul rolled the ball out to Yohan Cabaye, who pushed it forward to Hatem Ben Arfa, who was just inside his own half. Beating Sam Ricketts with a quick turn, he then sped off down the middle of the pitch with Bolton players unable to halt his progress, as if stunned by the audacity and brilliance of the run. Ignoring team mates left and right, Hatem made it into the box before delightfully slipping the ball into the net. The stadium erupted with noise (and head shaking), many fans not quite believing what they had just witnessed.

PAPISS CISSÉ v CHELSEA A, 2/5/12

United had never won at Stamford Bridge in the Premier League but Papiss Cissé was soon to put an end to that curse. His first goal on a memorable West London night came on 19 minutes. Davide Santon made progress down the left flank and played the ball infield as José Bosingwa tried to close him down. The ball found Papiss Cissé just inside the area and he then brilliantly flicked the ball up with his right foot before arrowing home an unstoppable left-footed volley into the top corner of the net. Terry and co could only stand and admire the strike.

PAPISS CISSÉ v CHELSEA A, 2/5/12

Into injury time and Ryan Taylor's throw-in down the United left was chested back by Shola Ameobi into the path of Papiss Cissé. With hardly a thought, Cissé, knowing exactly where the goal was, hit the most stupendous and unstoppable banana shot that flew off the outside of his right boot and beyond the despairing Petr Cěch. Didier Drogba had a look of stunned admiration on his face whilst Cěch simply didn't know what had hit him, the most incredible goal he has ever conceded.

Peter Beardsley's *Memoirs*

One of the most eminent of men to have played for the club in its long history. A brilliant little player, slight of build, who in his role operating just behind the front strikers proved devastating at both creating and scoring goals. Possessing lovely ball skills and marvellous vision, as well as tremendous stamina, enthusiasm and work-rate, above all Beardsley had the special quality of finding the net with truly spectacular goals, many coming from stunning long range shooting, splendid placement, precision timing or delightful dribbles.

After a period on trial at St. James' Park as a teenager, Peter also had spells with Gillingham, Cambridge United, Burnley and Oxford before he was picked up by former Newcastle skipper Bob Moncur, manager at Carlisle. He played one League Cup game for Manchester United, sandwiched between spells at Vancouver Whitecaps, before Arthur Cox brought him back to Tyneside to partner Kevin Keegan as Newcastle made sure they returned to Division One in spectacular fashion in 1984.

Looking back on that 1983/84 season, Peter says; *"Signing for Newcastle United was a dream come true for me and to play with such great players was a real thrill for me. I managed 20 goals during the season, which pleased me greatly, and if I had to pick a couple of stand out ones, then probably the one at Portsmouth which involved me beating a couple of players on the byline before shooting past Alan Knight and then the chip over Brighton's Joe Corrigan in the final game of the season."*

Beardsley's captivating brand of football matured and he became an England regular, an effective partner to Gary Lineker and he played in the final stages of two World Cups, in 1986 and 1990.

"The World Cup experience was magical", Peter recalls. "It was fantastic to get in the squad for the Mexico World Cup in 1986 and to score against Paraguay in the last 16 was unbelievable. We lost to Argentina in the quarter finals and that of course was the game memorable for Diego Maradona's two goals, the first his dubious handball, the second, one of the best individual goals I have had the privilege to see. In Italy four years later we really thought we had a good crack at winning the tournament but losing to West Germany on penalties in the semi-final was one of the most disappointing moments I have ever felt in football.

Harking back though, as a player you never forget your first cap or first goal. Mine came in 1986 against Egypt and Mexico respectively and they are days that are imprinted in your memory forever."

Tino Asprilla, Les Ferdinand and David Ginola were
out of this world and of course the following season
Alan Shearer joined us for a record £15m. They were
truly great days, and very happy ones too."

Now United's Football Development Manager,
Peter, who won 59 England caps (scoring 9 goals)
was awarded the MBE for his services to football
in 1995. Totalling 326 appearances for the Magpies,
and scoring 119 goals, Peter, to many United
supporters of the modern generation, is recognised
as the best player to have pulled on the black and
white shirt.

Back on the domestic front, Peter left United for
Anfield in search of trophies for a new British record
deal in 1986 and honours duly came. Beardsley was
noted as one of the country's top entertainers, and
after four years on the red side of Liverpool, he
moved across Stanley Park to Everton where he
again became a crowd favourite.

"My time on Merseyside was fantastic and
 was lucky enough to play with some great
names such as John Barnes, Alan Hansen and
Neville Southall", smiled Peter. "Winning the
League Championship twice and the FA Cup were
magical moments at Liverpool and although there
were no trophies at Goodison Park, I thoroughly
enjoyed my time there too."

When Beardsley was 32 years old, he made a
dramatic return to St. James Park for £1.5m, a fee
which proved to be the bargain of the decade. Back
alongside Kevin Keegan and later Arthur Cox too,
Peter led United's charge on the Premiership as he
enjoyed a new lease of life, skippering the Magpies
as they became a new force in the game.

"The media called us the 'Entertainers' and that
wasn't far from the truth. We finished third in our
first season back in the big time but I guess it was the
1995/96 season that most people will remember; so
close to winning the league, but yet so far. Players like

Snakes and Ladders

Newcastle United – European Campaign

70	69	68 Agonising extra time defeat	67	66	65 Late for training, go back 4 spaces	64
57	58	59	60	61	62	63 Concede penalty, go back 4 spaces
56	55	54 Head crucial late winner, advance 5 spaces	53	52	Booked 51	50
43	44	45 Hit superb hat-trick	46	47	48	49
42 Suffer bad injury	41 Deadline day new signing	40 Lost passport, go back 5 spaces	39	38	37	36
29	30	31	32	33	34 Win Penalty Shoot Out	35
28 Sign boot deal, advance 3 spaces	27	26	25	24	23	22
15	16	17	18 Club fine. Go back to square 9	19	20	21
14 Win Group Stage, advance 3 spaces	13	12	11	10 Win on Away Goals	9	8
1	2	3	4 Named club captain	5	6	7 Own goal horror - go back to start

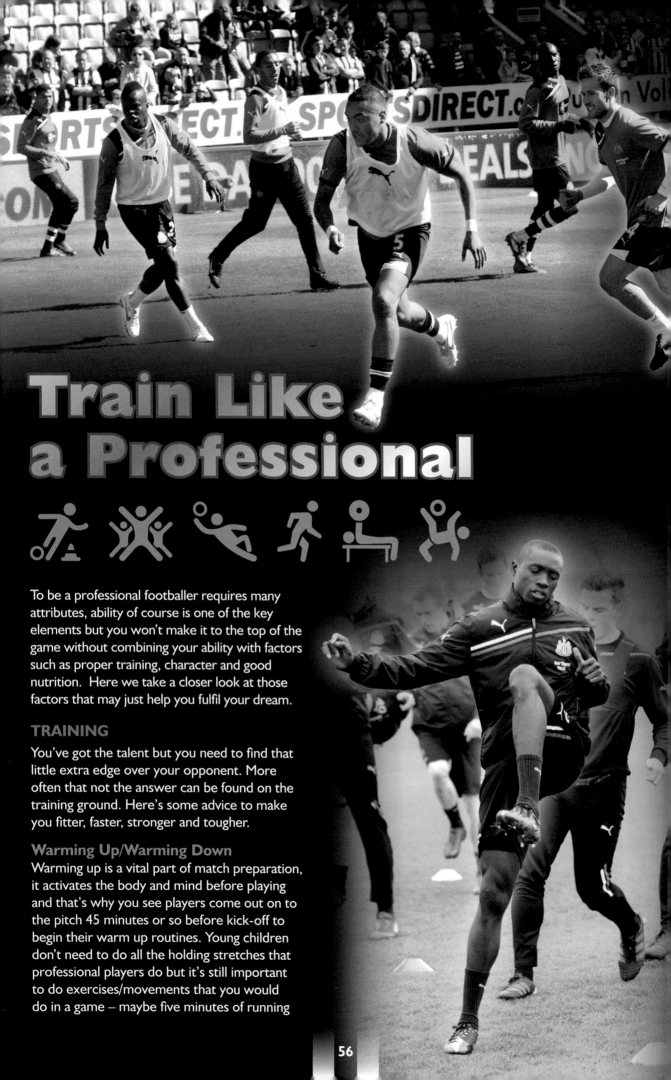

Train Like a Professional

To be a professional footballer requires many attributes, ability of course is one of the key elements but you won't make it to the top of the game without combining your ability with factors such as proper training, character and good nutrition. Here we take a closer look at those factors that may just help you fulfil your dream.

TRAINING

You've got the talent but you need to find that little extra edge over your opponent. More often that not the answer can be found on the training ground. Here's some advice to make you fitter, faster, stronger and tougher.

Warming Up/Warming Down

Warming up is a vital part of match preparation, it activates the body and mind before playing and that's why you see players come out on to the pitch 45 minutes or so before kick-off to begin their warm up routines. Young children don't need to do all the holding stretches that professional players do but it's still important to do exercises/movements that you would do in a game – maybe five minutes of running

across the pitch, moving forwards, backwards and sideways, followed by some leg swings and groin stretches. Then it's a good idea to do some ball work, for example if you're a striker, get plenty of touches and practice your shooting. Do the things that are specific to your position. Finish off by getting your body ready for sprint work with three or four short sharp sprints over 10-15 metres.

For young players, the benefits of a warm down aren't that great but it's important for professional players as sometimes there's very little rest between games. Although not essential for youngsters, it at least gets you into a good habit for later in your career.

Improving Speed

This can be achieved by increasing your stride frequency. Doing drills like ladders or hopscotch exercises get your feet working at speed, and these should be done in different directions, not just straight lines. Working on your stride length will help too so work on short sharp sprints.

Endurance and Stamina

Fitness is different in various sports so in football for example you're better off doing repeated sprints over 20-30 seconds, having a short recovery and then going again. Try and get all the movements you do in a game into this training, rather than just doing laps of the pitch. One of the best things for endurance is small-sided games played at a high tempo and of course simply playing games is a great way to attain match fitness.

Strength Exercises

Using weights is a good way to build up strength for professionals but for young players, who don't need to build muscle bulk it's more about getting your muscles used to working. Gymnastic movements, like sit-ups, chin-ups and press-ups, where you're working your muscles against your body weight, are a good way of achieving this. Professional players use resistance bands or bungee cords and run against them in short bursts. It's useful to start this sort of training from a young age but remember to always try and repeat the movements you do in a game in your training.

Training/Resting

It is essential that you get rest, but at the same time there's nothing wrong with doing physical activity every day; that said you shouldn't play match football every day. Something like two games and three or four training sessions a week is about the right balance. That's just the football though, keep those gymnastic movements going every day and then maybe a little bit of swimming or tennis which will help develop your footwork.

CHARACTER

An essential part of being a good footballer, it takes hard work and determination to become a professional coupled with these elements/attributes.

Attitude

You must always give your best, even when things aren't going too well for you. A positive attitude and a strong determination to succeed will help develop a winning mentality.

Behaviour

Try and always lead by example and be the best person you can. Your behaviour off the pitch is as important as on it.

Communication

Be your own person but equally, listen to the advice given by your parents, teachers and coaches. Ask questions if you're not sure about anything.

Discipline

Always be punctual and prepared. That means turning up for training and matches on time. Respect the people you're with, the equipment you use and the places where you play.

Enthusiasm

Give your best at all times, on and off the pitch and always encourage others around you.

Fair Play

Learn to win and learn to lose; be magnanimous in victory and dignified in defeat. Respect your opponents and the match officials.

NUTRITION

Having a healthy balanced diet, including fluids, is very important for all professional athletes.

Food and fluids are needed by the body to provide energy, recovery after training or a match, fighting off infections, recovering from injury and keeping the body at the correct temperature in order to produce optimum performance.

Our bodies need different nutrients in different amounts. Too much or not enough of each nutrient can make us tired or overheat which may lead to poor performance. Carbohydrate is the nutrient generally needed in the largest amount by footballers as it provides a major source of energy for your muscles. Without it your muscles lose their sharpness and your legs in particular will feel 'heavy' during a game.

A balanced day should contain:

- Breakfast
- At least two 'balanced meals'
- Extra Fluids
- Extra snacks if required
- Five portions of a mix of fruit, vegetables and salad

A balanced week should contain:

- A variety of starchy carbohydrate foods (bread, rice, potato, pasta)
- Red meat no more than three times a week (beef, steak, sausage, burgers)
- Fish at least twice a week (mackerel, salmon, sardines, tuna)
- Vegetables at least three times a week (beans, chickpeas, three-bean rice salad, nuts)

2012/13 Barclays Premier League Fixtures

Date	Opposition	H/A	K-Off	Score
Sat 18 August	Tottenham H	H	5.30	
Sat 25 August	Chelsea	A	5.30	
Sun 2 September	Aston Villa	H	4.00	
Mon 17 September	Everton	A	8.00	
Sat 22 September	Norwich City	H	3.00	
Sat 29 September	Reading	A	3.00	
Sun 7 October	Manchester United	H	4.00	
Sun 21 October	Sunderland	A	1.30	
Sat 27 October	West Brom	H	3.00	
Sun 4 November	Liverpool	A	4.00	
Sat 10 November	West Ham United	H	3.00	
Sat 17 November	Swansea City	H	3.00	
Sat 24 November	Southampton	A	3.00	
Tues 27 November	Stoke City	A	7.45	
Sat 1 December	Wigan Athletic	H	3.00	
Sat 8 December	Fulham	A	3.00	
Sat 15 December	Manchester City	H	3.00	
Sat 22 December	Queens Park Rgrs	H	3.00	
Wed 26 December	Manchester United	A	3.00	
Sat 29 December	Arsenal	A	3.00	
Tues 1 January	Everton	H	3.00	
Sat 12 January	Norwich City	A	3.00	
Sat 19 January	Reading	H	3.00	
Tues 29 January	Aston Villa	A	7.45	
Sat 2 February	Chelsea	H	3.00	
Sat 9 February	Tottenham H	A	3.00	
Sat 23 February	Southampton	H	3.00	
Sat 2 March	Swansea City	A	3.00	
Sat 9 March	Stoke City	H	3.00	
Sat 16 March	Wigan Athletic	A	3.00	
Sat 30 March	Manchester City	A	3.00	
Sat 6 April	Fulham	H	3.00	
Sat 13 April	Sunderland	H	1.30	
Sat 20 April	West Brom	A	3.00	
Sat 27 April	Liverpool	H	3.00	
Sat 4 May	West Ham Utd	A	3.00	
Sun 12 May	Queens Park Rgrs	A	3.00	
Sun 19 May	Arsenal	H	3.00	

* Fixtures subject to change

It's a Goal!

Newcastle United scored some wonderful goals throughout the 2011/12 season, and some less pretty ones too, but regardless of how the ball enters the net, the celebrations afterwards are usually much the same – great joy, passion and excitement as these pictures show in fabulous detail.

Arsenal

Wolves

Bolton

Liverpool

NEWCASTLE UNITED

Chelsea

Manchester United

Norwich

Stoke

Sunderland

61

PAGE 21

Quiz 1

What do you remember about the 2010/11 season?

1. Daniel Agger (og) at Anfield
2. Brighton
3. Demba Ba (v Blackburn)
4. Lille
5. Gervinho (Arsenal)
6. Manchester City, Arsenal and Tottenham
7. Bolton, Blackburn and Stoke
8. Frank Lampard and David Dunn
9. Wigan
10. Manchester City

Quiz 2

See how much you know about Newcastle United past and present

1. 2005 (FA Cup Semi Final v Man Utd)
2. Tottenham
3. West Ham
4. Manchester City
5. Feyenoord
6. Scotland
7. Chile
8. Freiburg
9. Manchester United
10. Didi Hamann

PAGE 39

```
        C A C A   P A              H
              E                    I
  T       P E A R C E              S
  O           C   D               L
A M E O B I   H   G               O
  A         B   H A R P E R
  S O L A N O   R         O
  S         U           W B
G O M   A     M O N C U R E
  N     L     S     L     R
        L   F O X   A     T
        E         R
        N         K
```

PAGE 41

PAGE 44

PAGE 45

1. Sammy Ameobi
2. Steven Taylor
3. Sylvain Marveaux
4. Mike Williamson
5. Fabricio Coloccini
6. Davide Santon
7. Yohan Cabaye
8. Tim Krul
9. Hatem Ben Arfa
10. Alan Pardew
11. Shola Ameobi
12. Cheick Tiote
13. Dan Gosling
14. Ryan Taylor
15. James Perch